IN THE WINGS

BEHIND THE SCENES at the
NEW YORK CITY BALLET

KYLE FROMAN

LINCOLN CENTER for the Performing Arts

John Wiley & Sons, Inc.

For Andrew

Published by John Wiley & Sons, Inc., Hoboken, New Jersey
Published simultaneously in Canada

Wiley Bicentennial Logo: Richard J. Pacifico

Design and composition by Navta Associates, Inc.

For general information about our other products and services, please contact our Customer Care Department within the United States at (800) 762-2974, outside the United States at (317) 572-3993 or fax (317) 572-4002.

Wiley also publishes its books in a variety of electronic formats. Some content that appears in print may not be available in electronic books. For more information about Wiley products, visit our web site at www.wiley.com.

Library of Congress Cataloging-in-Publication Data:

Froman, Kyle, 1976–
  In the wings : behind the scenes at the New York City Ballet / Kyle Froman.
     p. cm.
   ISBN 978-0-470-17343-5 (cloth)
 1. New York City Ballet—Anecdotes. 2. New York City Ballet—Pictorial works. 3. Froman, Kyle, 1976—Anecdotes. I. Title.
   GV1786.N4F76 2007
   792.809747'1—dc22   2007024556

Printed in China

10 9 8 7 6 5 4 3 2 1

Contents

Peter Martins rehearses a child for Mozartiana. *Choreography by George Balanchine.*

Foreword

by Peter Martins

Ballet Master in Chief,
New York City Ballet

COUNTLESS PHOTOGRAPHERS HAVE SPENT THEIR CAREERS SHOOTING dance, often at the New York City Ballet. The one thing virtually all of them have in common is that they've aimed their lenses from the audience.

The photographs in this book are different. When Kyle Froman set out to document the NYCB, he was like a wartime photographer embedded with the troops. His pictures give witness to the advances—and the "casualties"— of a season in the life of our company.

Only a dancer could have accomplished this so successfully. Only a dancer in the company would have such unparalleled access. And only a dancer would have such a finely tuned instinct for how to use it.

Kyle is a child of the NYCB. Like many of our dancers, he joined us at a young age and in a real way grew up here. For more than a decade, he has spent twelve hours a day inside the walls of Lincoln Center, studying under the tutelage of some of the great masters of the ballet world. Like his colleagues, he's eaten and sometimes slept here, celebrated milestones here, laughed and probably cried here. His family consists of one hundred of the world's most gifted dancers, many of them younger than thirty. Most of them can describe every inch of the New York State Theater and every step of choreography in a hundred different ballets.

That's the background that Kyle brought to his journey into photography. It all started very quietly: one day he showed up for company class with a camera slung over his sweatshirt. After his own rehearsals ended, he'd sit on the floor cross-legged and shoot his colleagues. Soon, he and his camera became a common sight around the theater. He was photographing his fellow dancers inside the makeup room, in wardrobe, in the physical therapy room. And at each night's performance, it seemed, he was in the wings, shooting our productions from behind the scenes. Anyone else would have been perceived as a voyeur. But Kyle is a member of the family. And so we just went about our business.

When he brought his work to show me for the first time, I was impressed. It was a stunning marriage of photojournalism and art. The view he presented of our dancers was unusually intimate, and often raw in its honesty. But there was also an unmistakable feeling of love.

His perspective was familiar to me: when I joined the New York City Ballet as a young dancer, I used to stand in the wings every night, watching the world's greatest repertory. There's something extraordinary about watching these ballets being performed close-up; no house seat can compare to what you see from there. The photographs offered a glimpse of a world the public almost never gets to see.

It became clear that Kyle's gift for dance was just part of a larger artistic sensibility (which isn't so unusual—some of our dancers have become choreographers and even composers). We gave him his own section on our company Web site, and started publishing his photos in our literature. It was just a matter of time before he was offered an opportunity to showcase his work in a book.

Here is New York City Ballet as it really is—the good, the not so good, and the majestically beautiful. It's a true story, and it's told by someone who can honestly claim that he was there.

Acknowledgments

WHEN I BEGAN THIS PROJECT OF DOCUMENTING MY LIFE AS A DANCER in the New York City Ballet, I wasn't sure what would come of it. If a book was to be possible, I knew I needed everyone's cooperation to succeed. But with so many trusts, unions, and dancers involved, I thought for sure the project would be squashed along the way.

The fact that this book was made says a lot about the people I'm lucky to be surrounded by. Maybe it's our common goal of creating beauty that allows us to trust each other. Whatever the reason, thank you all for allowing me to go forward with it. I'm eternally grateful to everyone who made this book possible.

First, let me thank Peter Martins, Christopher Ramsey, Holly Hynes, Robert Daniels, and Ken Tabachnick from the New York City Ballet. Your encouragement has meant everything to me. Thank you for letting me show our company to the world.

Another thanks to both Ellen Sorrin, from the Balanchine Trust, and Christopher Pennington, from the Jerome Robbins Trust. These ballets are our lives, and we have this in common. Thank you for letting these master-pieces live in my book as they do onstage.

Stage manager Perry Silvey and the New York State Theater stage crew have been especially great. I'm sure I've made their lives crazy the past year, crawling in the wings to get the shots I want, but I hope they agree the aggravation was worth it. Also, thank you to Mike Wekselblatt and IATSE/Local One.

I'd like to thank my agent, Lynn Seligman, for believing in my project, for sticking in there through thick and thin. Also, thank you to my editor, Hana Lane, and to John Wiley & Sons for giving "my baby" a home.

I'd like to thank the entire Froman family and the entire Kirtzman family. I'm lucky to have such beautiful and loving people in my life.

Thank you to my mother, Sally Froman, for making me believe I could do anything. I love you with all my heart. Thank you to my first ballet teacher, my sister Debbi Jo, who started me on this path and made dancing fun every step of the way. Also, to my twin, Kurt, thank you for holding my hand through life.

Another thank-you to my husband, Andrew Kirtzman. Thank you for your encouragement every step of the way. Thank you for loving me. You're a dream come true.

Finally, a special thank-you to the dancers of the New York City Ballet, past and present. You will always inspire me.

INTRODUCTION

As a dancer, I've often felt the view behind the scenes was more interesting than the finished product. With all the daily injuries, cast changes, and lack of rehearsal time, it can be amazing that our shows make it to the stage.

Ultimately, it's up to the dancers to pull the show off. Our daily routine trains us to be up for this challenge. It also trains us to be who we are—artists—and it's in the rehearsal hall, not just onstage, where our art is created. Our home, the New York State Theater, has no windows, but I hope this book can be a window into our lives.

The New York City Ballet was the only company I ever wanted to join. As a teenager in Texas, I discovered the choreographic genius of George

Balanchine. I learned that his company was the New York City Ballet, and that it was the best. Joining the NYCB immediately became my goal, and I achieved it just a few years later.

I've been given a wonderful life. The past eleven years have been packed with dancing, international tours, and television and film appearances. I studied with wonderful teachers at the School of American Ballet, and I performed with some of the last generation of dancers handpicked by Balanchine.

After so many years with the NYCB, I thought I'd seen it all. But when I started photographing the company, looking through the camera lens brought me back to when I first became part of it.

The daily moments I'd been taking for granted started revealing themselves in the pictures I'd taken around the theater. I saw with fresh eyes the truly bizarre situations that nobody else in the world faces, as well as those transcendent moments that most people never experience.

I've always felt honored to be a dancer in the New York City Ballet. Now I feel privileged to show this life to others. These are the world's finest dancers, and this is a chronicle of their struggles for perfection, and sometimes their struggles just to make it through the season able to walk.

10:15 A.M.

Sewing shoes before company class.

WALKING INTO THE STUDIO BEFORE COMPANY CLASS is hard for me these days. It's not the thought of working that bothers me, it's the realization that so much has changed in such a small amount of time. I've been in the New York City Ballet for eleven years, and the company now hardly

Megan LeCrone pins up her hair.

resembles the company I joined. I always expected there to be turnover, with older dancers being replaced by younger ones. I just wasn't expecting to feel so old this quickly.

As I walk through the maze of dancers stretching on the floor and barres that have been pulled to the center of the room, I spot a space far away from the mirror. The studio is filled with chatter about last night's show. Apparently a dancer sprained her ankle, and the schedule for today has changed in order to replace her for tonight's show. Thankfully, I'm not affected.

A tattooed dancer.

The number of people who have chosen to take class today is impressive, but the fact that they've made it into the studio before me is disconcerting. It's clear to me they've been here awhile, as I watch them complete their morning rituals of abdominal exercises and stretches. The girls are sewing ribbons on their new pointe shoes. They've already rolled their muscles out on foam rollers and massaged themselves by lying on rubber balls. Now, they're completely prepared to look their best.

As I walk through the studio to the barre I eye the younger generation. They seem much more sure of themselves than I was at their age. I wonder what they think of me and the other senior dancers. Do they think we're old, or bitter? Do they like our dancing, or do they wonder how we managed to

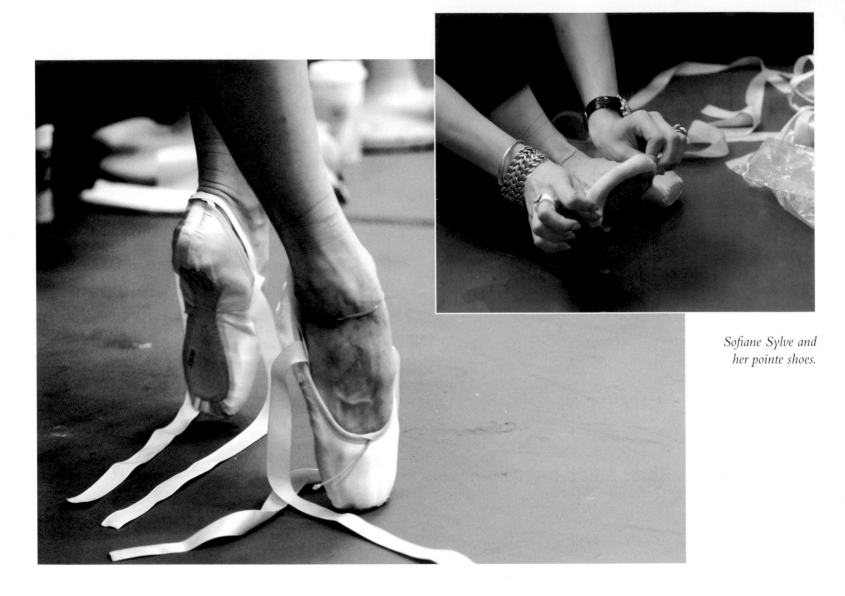

*Sofiane Sylve and
her pointe shoes.*

6

Savannah Lowery preparing her shoes.

Another barre begins.

get into the company? There's an obvious generation gap that hasn't been bridged.

Each dancer has a different routine before class. Some show up to the studio an hour early to stretch and warm up, while others stroll into class five minutes late, cup of coffee in hand. Though class is designed to prepare a dancer's body for the day's dancing, a pre–warm-up is usually necessary. Even for the most coordinated and flexible dancer, ballet feels very unnatural at ten o'clock in the morning.

Merrill Ashley teaching class.

I usually give myself a good two and a half hours to get to the studio early, but I can't seem to make it in time to warm up the way I used to. When I was a teenager in Texas, forty-five minutes of stretching before class was the norm for me. This was bizarre even to the girls I danced with. But after a long day of high school, I wanted my few hours of dancing to really count.

Three ballets go on tonight for the first time this season, which means that the rehearsal schedule for today is packed, taking up two pages on the bulletin board instead of the usual one. Though it was posted last night, dancers still crowd around it in disbelief. "I have five hours straight with no break," one dancer says to me. I'm involved with only Balanchine's *Square Dance*, but it happens to be one of the hardest ballets I've ever performed.

Sous-sus.

Abi Stafford.

I settle into my remote space at barre and run through my usual stretches in the remaining minutes before class starts. I layer on two pairs of sweatpants, throw on some leg warmers, and tie a sweatshirt around my waist. My legs feel like rocks from jumping in last night's performance.

With hope, the leg warmers will help loosen them up.

When I was a young dancer in the company, there was only one spot at barre for me. My chosen place to start class was closest to the mirror, just to the left of the door. Though some dancers like to feel their bodies instead of looking at them, this was a spot where I could keep an eye on my left side, my weak side. These days I'm more of a "feeling" kind of dancer. After all, there's no mirror onstage.

I think about Stanley Williams, my former teacher from the School of American Ballet, a lot in class, and I regret that this younger generation never knew him. I see him demonstrating barre exercises in his quiet way, and I hear his corrections to the class. He was the reason my twin brother, Kurt, and I moved up to New York from Texas. It was Stanley's decision to award us with the first Rudolf Nureyev scholarship. What he gave us set our lives on a wonderful course.

Grand battement.

Dancers changing shoes after barre.

Whenever I get to the studio early for class, so early that the lights are still half off, I think of my first few years in the company. On Tuesday mornings, Kurt and I would walk in to find Stanley at the piano stretching his calves. Tuesday was Stanley's day to teach company class. We'd say our hellos and chat for a while before he'd leave to smoke his pipe. I remember feeling such respect and love, not just for Stanley, but for what I did. I had so much to look forward to—ballets to dance, teachers to learn from.

The class starts right on time, always five minutes late. As people move through the positions of pliés I can hear the sounds of cracking hips and knees. It's the beginning of another day of rehearsals with the show looming at eight o'clock. I try not to think about the demands of *Square Dance* and just concentrate on getting my body going.

The music pouring from the piano charges the air, making my heart beat

Merrill Ashley demonstrates the combination.

15

faster. Along with the music, chitchat fills the room. With all of its rules and discipline, ballet can be hard for even ballet dancers to take seriously in the morning. Some dancers use class as an opportunity to sharpen their wit, practicing one-liners along with their tendus. I've definitely fallen in with this crowd.

I feel warmer with each passing combination at the barre. During a stretch forward at the end of ronde de jambes, I watch the sweat pool at my feet. It's time to take some clothing off. I strip off a layer and prepare to see more of what my body really looks like. I hope to be down to tights and a T-shirt by the end of class, but I continue to wear a pair of sweatpants for the rest of barre. I don't have the confidence to see my body just yet.

During the season, when rehearsal time is crucial, our morning company class is shortened from an hour and a half to just an hour. Though most dancers find class boring compared to the rest of their day, the abbreviated classes can cost you. There's no longer time to properly warm up for the day's work, no easing your body into ballet mode. As the season progresses, you get

Battement tendu.

OPPOSITE *Sofiane Sylve spins.*

16

Young students peek into company class.

into performance shape, which means you look good but feel awful. Before long you start missing those longer classes.

The barres are pushed toward the sides of the room, and center work begins. The volume in the room rises as dancers begin comparing notes on the class. Everything is up for criticism, from the pianist's choice of music to the teacher's combinations. The room feels emptier suddenly as several dancers pick up their bags and leave.

Jared Angle cabrioles, as Alan Moverman plays.

Fifteen minutes remain as we finish up the last of several turning combinations. I realize that a silence has overtaken the room, and all eyes are fixed on the best female "turners" in the company—Sofiane Sylve, Ashley Bouder, Jennie Somogyi, and Tiler Peck. They have claimed the floor and are having a turning contest. Each has added double and triple fouettés to the combination and is spinning like mad. They look like whirling dervishes, and the effect is mesmerizing.

The competition is a draw as all four girls finish perfectly. The abundance of talent in the company constantly amazes me.

Albert Evans.

As the class proceeds through jumps, Daniel Ulbricht catches my eye. Daniel is short for a male dancer, but his dancing is larger than life. His body is so strong and compact that the jumps and turns he can pull off are stunning. I'm flabbergasted as he adds beats to every jump in the petite allegro combination. His speed rivals even that of the girls in the company.

With only a combination or two left in class, I consider my day before deciding whether I should leave early and stretch on my own or stick it out through the rest of jumps. Since there's a lot of jumping in *Square Dance*,

I decide to be good and stay for the remaining combinations. It's a struggle to keep pushing, but I know I'll be thankful for it later. Jumping is a lot easier if I've been doing it all day, not just before the curtain goes up.

To outsiders, class is a spectacle. Dancers start the day with the smallest of movements, pliés. As the class progresses, the energy builds, the sweat pours. An hour later, dancers are literally flying through the air. Dancers don't appreciate the drama of it all. To us, it's just the beginning of another day.

Peter Martins walks into the room for the final few minutes of class. He

Seth Orza.

takes his usual seat by the piano and watches as he sips his coffee. The combinations at the end are always the hardest, mostly a manège or a tour en l'air.
These are my least favorite things to do in the morning.

I like it when Peter watches me in performance, but I feel ridden with
faults when he observes class. The usual question arises: Do I leave now or
risk messing up in front of him? The cup of coffee in his hand gives me my
answer, and I head off to the Starbucks across the street before rehearsal.

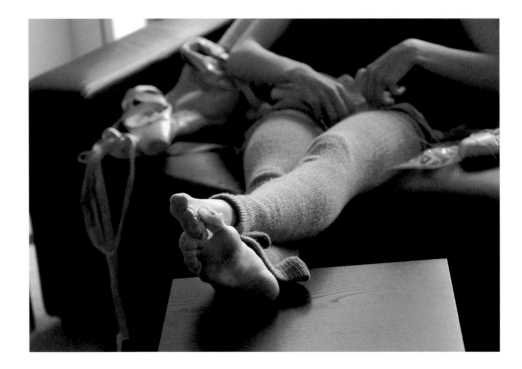

Sore feet.

Max van der Sterre stretches before class.

Ellen Bar prepares for class.

OPPOSITE
Dara Johnson.

Megan LeCrone.

Merrill Ashley.

Sofiane Sylve stretches her hips.

OPPOSITE *Sean Lavery teaching*
company class onstage.

11:30 A.M.

O N MY WAY DOWN TO MY DRESSING ROOM ON THE
third floor, I pass the physical therapy room. I catch
sight of Marika Molnar working on the dancer injured the
night before. The girl has obviously had a tearful night, and her
emotions are on edge as Marika tests her range of motion. If

Henry Blumenkranz
works on a dancer.

anyone can help this girl, it's Marika. She's a leader in the field of dance medicine and the founder of Westside Dance Physical Therapy.

New York City Ballet dancers carry such a physically demanding schedule that we quickly learn the necessity of maintenance. We have acupuncturists, massage therapists, chiropractors, and physical therapists at our disposal. They're very useful in helping us recover from injuries but invaluable in heading them off.

Injuries teach dancers about their bodies. Dancers learn their weak spots, their Achilles' heels, and they learn to stay on top of them. Also, injuries force dancers to reevaluate their technique and correct mistakes in their training. I always felt I improved more when I was injured than when I was performing every night of the season.

A "casualty."

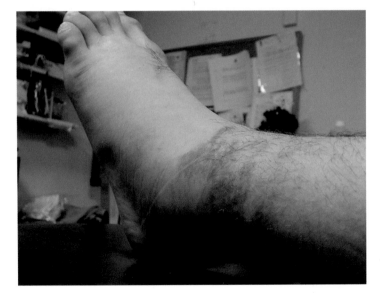

The massage therapist has arrived, and seeing that her table is free I decide to stop in for a quick psoas muscle release. As her fingers sink deep into my stomach, nausea sweeps over me. The first time I experienced this type of release work, I couldn't comprehend the need to release this muscle located deep within my core. I relented upon learning the effect it would have on everything from my breathing and balance to my

34

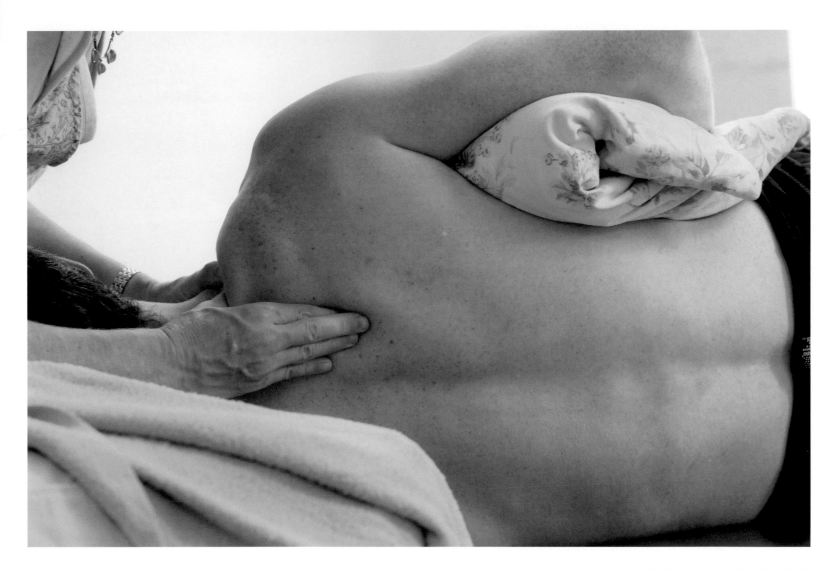

Seth Orza gets his shoulder fixed.

The laser.

alignment, back, and legs. The sensation was unbearable the first time. Now, I think it feels good. Dancers develop such an incredibly high pain threshold. Dancing can hurt, but the maintenance required after dancing can be even worse.

One thing dancers learn over the years is the need for balance in our muscles. We find we can't train with ballet only. If we did, we'd be constantly turning out our legs, arching our backs, pointing our feet. Before long, we'd start tearing our bodies apart.

For this reason, dancers supplement with other forms of exercise. Yoga is great for lengthening the body, opening up the back, and breathing.

OPPOSITE Henry Blumenkranz digs into Sofiane Sylve's calves.

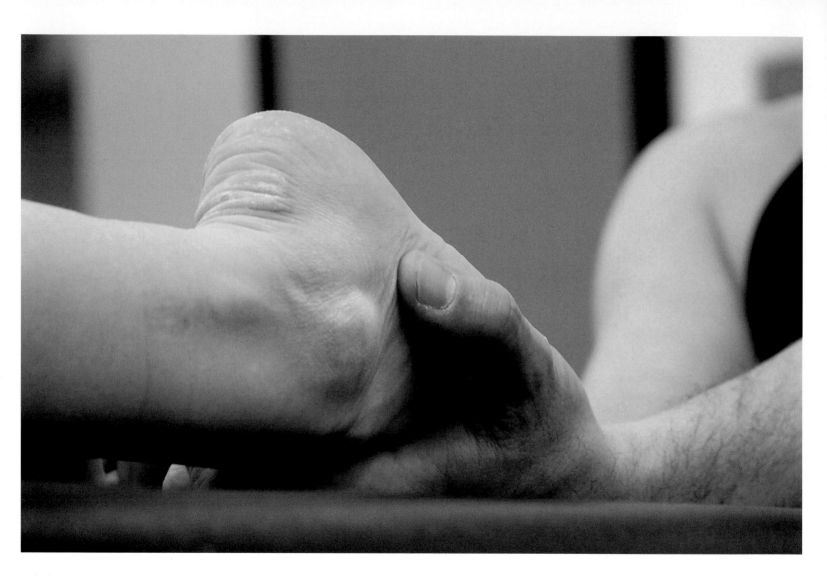

Likolani Brown.

Elliptical machines and stationary bikes allow us to exercise with our legs remaining parallel. Also, Pilates is a perfect supplemental exercise for dancers. It allows us to stretch, strengthen, and balance our bodies with an emphasis on alignment, core strength, control, and fluidity.

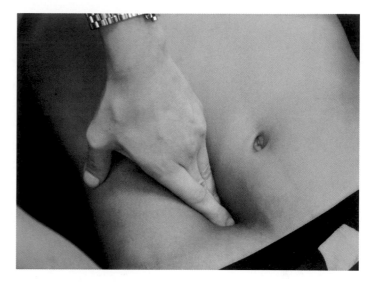

A psoas release.

Supplemental exercise can do wonders for our stamina. Over the last few years, I've discovered the benefits of cardiovascular training. Not only does it warm me up for class in the morning, but it helps get me through the hardest ballets, like tonight's *Square Dance*. Most people think dancers have incredible stamina, but the opposite is usually true. Almost all the work we do is start and stop. Usually, the only time we dance for twenty or thirty minutes in a row is during the performances at night. Even during the run-through rehearsals onstage, we usually stop for corrections. Cardio training really helps with this.

Halfway through my psoas release I zone out to the sound of Marika's voice. She diagnoses the girl's injury as only a first-degree sprain. The girl is lucky and should recover in a week or two. To be on the safe side, though, Marika recommends stopping in to see one of our orthopedic surgeons, Dr. Bauman and Dr. Hamilton, for an X-ray.

Our physical therapy room in the theater is incredibly small. It's barely large enough for two examination tables, but somehow there's room for all the machines that keep us going. We have electrical stimulation machines, for contracting specific muscles and promoting healing; a refresh roller, which is used to massage calves and feet; an ultrasound machine, which promotes healing and circulation while shrinking swelling; and even a laser, used for pain relief and for speeding up the healing process. A common sight in the PT room is a dancer or two connected to wires.

As my time on the table runs out, I think about my rehearsal schedule for the afternoon, a run-through of *Square Dance* onstage, with Peter watching. If the psoas release didn't make me feel nauseated enough, the thought of rehearsing *Square Dance* full-out in the afternoon and performing it again tonight does the job. I try to reassure myself by concentrating on how I've danced the ballet for many years and know the parts to rest in, but I know that nothing will make me feel less nervous. I just have to do it.

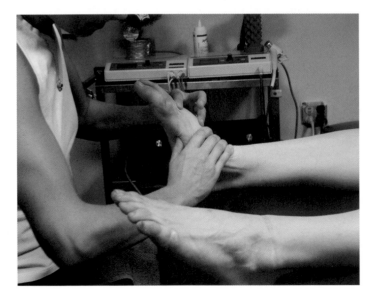

Therapist Michelle Rodriguez works on a foot.

Square Dance premiered in 1957, with Patricia Wilde and Nicholas Magallanes as the lead couple. It went through two different incarnations, originally having a caller and an orchestra onstage. It's very fast, packed with jumps, and the corps de ballet hardly gets to leave the stage. It's

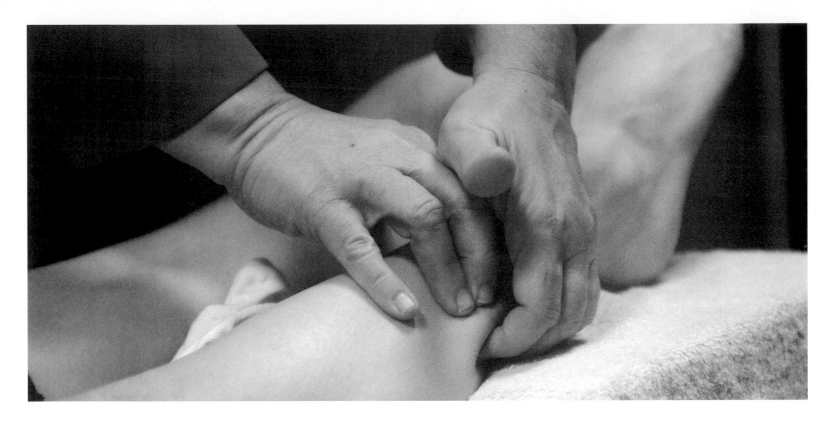

hard stamina-wise, but as the curtain comes down, you feel that you've really accomplished something.

There's just enough time to run across the street for a sandwich before my two o'clock rehearsal. Thankfully, this is my only rehearsal today, and the fact that there's time to go home and even take a short nap before the show calms my nerves. I say my good-byes in the therapy room and head downstairs to strip off my sweaty clothes.

Marika Molnar's hands.

2:15 P.M.

THE NEW YORK STATE THEATER HAS TWO STUDIOS ON the fifth floor: the main hall and the practice room. The main hall is where we take class every morning. After the years of emergency rehearsals, the choreographing of new ballets, and the sweat I've spilled there, I'm surprised I still have good

Ana Sophia Scheller rehearses The Nutcracker. *Choreography by George Balanchine.*

feelings about this studio. But there's a sense of history you can feel as soon as you walk in. I've seen photographs of Balanchine and Jerry Robbins choreographing ballets in this room. The essence of all this dancing permeates the walls.

Since the main hall is the same size as the stage, most ballets are rehearsed here before they make it downstairs. The rehearsals that stick in my mind over the years are definitely the run-throughs of our story ballets, *The*

Balanchine's Serenade.

Before a rehearsal.

Wendy Whelan and Nikolaj Hübbe in a run-through for The Sleeping Beauty. *Choreography by Peter Martins.*

Nutcracker, Coppélia, The Sleeping Beauty, and *Swan Lake*. The casts for these are normally huge, complete with children from the School of American Ballet. There's a dramatic energy that builds in these rehearsals. All eyes are on you when you're dancing, and they can make you feel naked. Sometimes they add to the magic of your dancing; sometimes they see every mistake.

Sean Lavery rehearses Sara Mearns and Stephen Hanna for Symphony in C. *Choreography by George Balanchine.*

They even watch during the corrections you might get after you've danced. The stress level is even higher in these run-throughs than during performances. When you're performing onstage in front of two thousand people, you can't see them watching you.

The practice room is another story. Roughly a third the size of the stage, it's used for smaller rehearsals. Dancing in there feels like dancing in a large closet. The floor is in need of an upgrade, and the walls are still painted a claustrophobic blue-gray. Sometimes a larger rehearsal takes over this studio, and if you dance on the sides it's a nightmare. There's either a piano or a video cart in the way. It is intimate, though, and it's directly across from the therapy room, a good place to rehearse if you have a massage afterward.

We're fifteen minutes into our stage rehearsal for *Square Dance*. Rosemary Dunleavy, the head ballet mistress, and Peter are still incorporating the principal dancers, Miranda Weese and Sébastien Marcovici, into the ballet. Except in extremely rare circumstances, the corps and the principals have separate rehearsals and usually see each other only for final run-throughs. This allows the ballet to be taught more efficiently, with the corps learning the steps and formations and the leads getting more specific instruction. The principals normally have more time to prepare their parts, and their coaching is more hands-on with the ballet mistress. Since the corps dancers are normally busy with lots of other ballets, the luxury of this type of rehearsal isn't an option. Also, the sheer number of corps dancers in most ballets makes one-on-one coaching unrealistic.

This first run-through is just for our spacing. The minute we're done

OPPOSITE The corps de ballet from Serenade. *Choreography by George Balanchine.*

48

setting the ballet onstage we'll go back to the beginning and rehearse full-out with lights. We won't hear the orchestra until the show tonight.

Whether a ballet gets lighting, costume, and orchestra rehearsals depends on various factors. Normally, the more complicated the music, the better the chance for a rehearsal with the orchestra. A ballet like Balanchine's *Episodes* always gets one, but *Square Dance* never does, because the music is easy for

Symphony in
Three Movements.
*Choreography by
George Balanchine.*

50

Susan Hendl coaches Andrew Veyette and Miranda Weese.

Marika Anderson dances Serenade. *Choreography by George Balanchine.*

OPPOSITE *Sara Mearns rehearses*
Swan Lake *at Saratoga Performing Arts*
Center. Choreography by Peter Martins.

the dancers to hear. The same holds true for costumes. If there are quick costume changes, the costumes are hard to move in, or the ballet is new and needs to be lit, then a dress rehearsal is required. Leotard ballets like *Agon*, *Stravinsky Violin Concerto*, and *Symphony in Three Movements* are never rehearsed in costume, because the costumes are so basic.

For dancers, there is nothing so transporting as hearing the orchestra for

Swan Lake *from above. Choreography by Peter Martins.*

Maria Kowroski, Stephen Hanna, and Miranda Weese rehearse Serenade. *Choreography by George Balanchine.*

Wendy Whelan and Nikolaj Hübbe.

the first time and feeling the stage lights electrifying the stage. The over-whelming buzz we feel when everything finally comes together makes the tedious rehearsals before worth it.

As the real run-through takes off, nervous energy fills my gut. The beginning of the ballet always does this to me. It's like the beginning of a marathon. I love *Square Dance*, but it takes every bit of concentration not to

Sean Lavery and Sterling Hyltin in a rehearsal for Duo Concertant. *Choreography by George Balanchine.*

Rosemary Dunleavy rehearsing the different casts of "Chinese" from
The Nutcracker. *Choreography by George Balanchine.*

OPPOSITE *Wendy Whelan and Sébastien
Marcovici working on* After the Rain.
Choreography by Christopher Wheeldon.

be scared of getting tired. I think my partner, Pauline Golbin, feels exactly
the same. We end up looking into each other's eyes a lot, exchanging moral
support and encouraging words while tackling the steps. Pauline's been in the
corps even longer than I have. We've endured our years in the company, and
we share this special feeling when we dance together.

Susan Hendl watches Janie Taylor and Sébastien Marcovici rehearse their pas de deux from Ecstatic Orange. *Megan LeCrone and Ask la Cour understudy. Choreography by Peter Martins.*

Jean-Pierre Frohlich demonstrates during a rehearsal for The Cage. *Choreography by Jerome Robbins.*

As good as it is experiencing the struggle of *Square Dance* with Pauline, there's nothing like finishing this hard ballet. It's ultimately more gratifying than anything. Your emotions become so heightened onstage that the accomplishment you feel by pushing through the fear and exhaustion is empowering.

The principals dart out onstage. I love Miranda and Sébastien as the lead couple, and since this is just a rehearsal, I turn my head and watch them more than I normally would. Miranda's dancing is calm and clear, and physically she's gorgeous. Halfway through the ballet, as I'm doubled over panting, I watch her lead the "Girls' Dance." She's going to be great tonight. Just before the lightning-speed finale, the corps finally gets to leave the stage for the principal man's solo. We're barely in the wings before we collapse. Breathless groans escape as we try to rejuvenate our bodies in the few minutes before our re-entrance, the final push of the ballet.

Some dancers stretch their hamstrings on the barres offstage, while others simply lie on their backs and shake their legs above them. "That was hard," says Troy Schumacher. He lies down next to me as he rubs his calves. "I watched all the other guys standing on the side to make sure I wasn't the only one who was breathing hard." Troy has been in the company a year, and

Dancers on a five-minute break.

I think he's a talented dancer. He's young, but he's very smart. Tonight is his first *Square Dance*.

I think of any words of wisdom to pass on. "Breathe as much as you can before the 'Boys' Dance' starts," I tell him. "Also, try to have fun. It makes it easier."

From my place on the floor I can hear that the music has stopped. "Can this be any faster?" Sébastien asks Maurice Kaplow, the conductor, who is

Wendy Whelan and Nikolaj Hübbe in a Main Hall run-through of The Nutcracker. *Choreography by George Balanchine.*

Sara Mearns rehearses off of a videotape.

Ecstatic Orange, *with Janie Taylor and Sébastien Marcovici. Choreography by Peter Martins.*

sitting next to the pianist. Sébastien is having a problem with the slow pirou-ettes in his solo. It's a hard step because the turns have to be fluid and calm, but if the tempo is too slow, it can be impossible not to hop in them. Maury adjusts the tempo accordingly, but the turns are still a problem. I can see that Sébastien is getting frustrated. "They'll be fine tonight," he tells Peter.

OPPOSITE
Rebecca Krohn and
Sébastien Marcovici.

Jean-Pierre Frohlich coaching Robbins's The Cage.

As Sébastien's solo ends, the corps takes its place in the wings. We give one another the thumbs-up across the stage before we step out onstage. The end is in sight.

The music is incredibly fast for the finale, and I love it that way. The boys turn away from their girls and do a pirouette combination facing the audience. I can feel that the boy next to me is way too close, and as we take off for our turns again, his hand smacks my hand. I double over, gripping my throbbing fingers to my chest. "I'm sorry! Are you okay?" he asks as he continues to dance. I'm so stunned I can barely breathe.

I move into the wings to avoid the scampering dancers and try to move my swelling knuckles. I can tell they're not broken, but I also know that this isn't nothing. They feel as if they were bent backwards when we hit, and suddenly the thought crosses my mind, "Am I out?"

Being "out" means being injured, out of commission, and it can be devastating. We train all day, every day. We have ballets we're looking forward to,

Rosemary Dunleavy setting the first movement of Balanchine's Vienna Waltzes *onstage.*

Ashley Laracey.

a schedule to live by. Then, suddenly—which is how big injuries tend to happen—you're out. You don't know for how long or if it's career-ending. In most instances, for the first few days you're in incredible pain, stuck at home with a bag of ice numbing whatever you've done to yourself. Your season could be over on the first day.

Merrill Ashley coaching
Sofiane Sylve.

The first time I went out was during my third year in the company. In a performance of *West Side Story Suite*, I fell forward while doing a knee-spin at the end of "Cool." Instinctively, I put a hand out to catch myself, jamming my left thumb into the stage. I remember going to bed that night hoping I'd just sprained it, all the while knowing I'd felt the dreaded "pop" when it happened.

It turned out to be a torn ligament and a fracture. I had no idea how to react, especially because the rest of me was fine. It was my thumb that was keeping me off the stage, and I felt guilty. I stayed at the theater the whole next day trying to help teach dancers my parts. In hindsight, I should have just left it up to the ballet masters to teach the understudies. I remember a few of them getting annoyed with my input. New York City Ballet is like a machine, and it works best when you stay out of its way.

A dancer can also go out when small or chronic injuries become unbearable. Tendinitis, strains, ribs out of place—these can be worse than tears and fractures. Small injuries can actually take longer to heal than big ones. Emotionally they're much harder to deal with, because dancers have to make a choice of how long to keep going. Dancers either think, "I'll just push through; I don't want to inconvenience anyone with emergency rehearsals to replace me," or they swallow their pride and admit they can't go on.

Rosemary comes over to me as the other dancers are finishing the finale of *Square Dance*. She asks what happened, and I tell her, "It wasn't his fault. We

OPPOSITE
Sara Mearns.

were too close." I assure her I'll be fine, when really I'm running through the ballet in my head, searching for partnering I do with that hand. There are a few fast lifts, but I'll worry about those later.

I ask to be excused to have Marika look at it and then race upstairs to find her in the physical therapy room. I practically jump out of my skin as she gently touches the ligaments on either side of my two middle fingers. I

Peter Martins, Yvonne Borree, and Nikolaj Hübbe in a rehearsal for Duo Concertant. *Choreography by George Balanchine.*

Sébastien Marcovici dances "Melancholic" in a run-through of The Four Temperaments. *Choreography by George Balanchine.*

worry, suddenly reliving the *West Side Story* injury, but Marika diagnoses this as just a sprain and tells me there's nothing more I can do than ice it.

I head down to the dressing room I share with ten other senior corps and soloist men. I strip off my clothes with one hand and then attempt to get dressed in street clothes the same way. This proves more difficult. Fifteen minutes later I'm back at the deli across the street buying another sandwich and water for now and a Coke for before the show. I'm no longer going home for my nap. I'm exhausted emotionally and physically, but there's a bed in our dressing room, and it's beckoning me.

Austin Laurent.

6:15 P.M.

DANCERS ARE INCREDIBLY SUPERSTITIOUS, ESPECIALLY before shows. I'm not sure if it's the anxiety surrounding performances or if we're all just crazy, but our habits come out at night. Most people just cross themselves, but one dancer I know picks up lint off the stage and puts it in his costume for good luck. My particular weird habit is how I get into my costume. I sit in my chair and put my tights, sock, and shoe on my right side before I do the left. I don't know why. It makes me feel that I'll have a good show, so I keep doing it.

I'm normally the first one in the dressing room getting ready. My friends don't get it, but I'd rather be early and calm than late and rushed. As I finish sewing elastics onto a pair of shoes, my best friend and fellow corps dancer Craig Hall comes in from a rehearsal. He collapses at his spot and watches as I start my makeup. Excitedly, he puts on the latest podcast of a comedian

Dressing room.

OPPOSITE
A sweaty dancer.

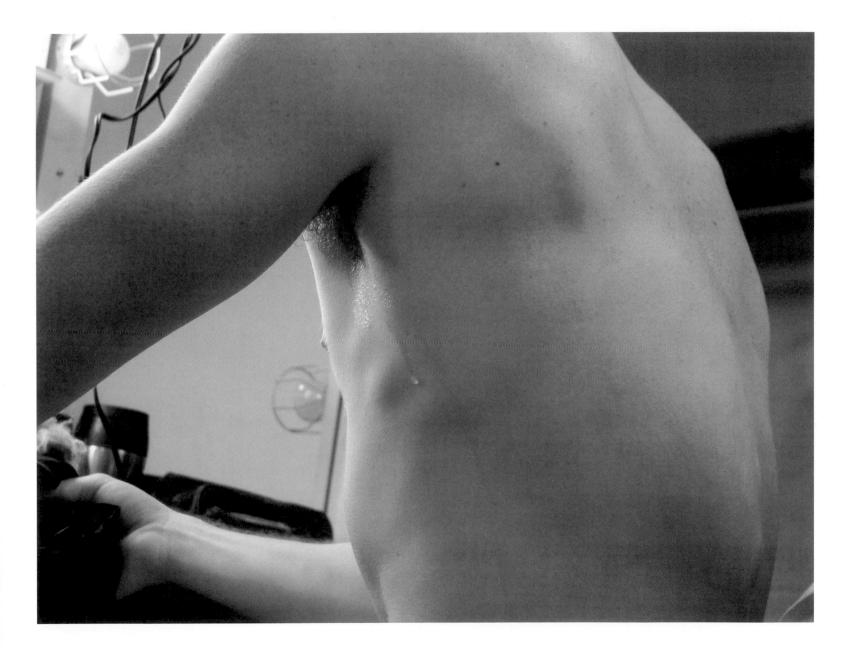

Seth Orza.

he has discovered, and the dressing room comes to life. Other dancers come in with their huge dinners to listen. Henry Seth, a friend since my SAB days, eats Chinese food, while Seth Orza, a talented and handsome dancer, eats a burrito. I'm suddenly starving, but I could never eat so much food before a show, much less before wearing a leotard.

Sean Suozzi and Tyler Angle, both great dancers and close friends, must have heard the podcast in their dressing room, because they come running in. "Play it again. Start it over," says Sean, as Tyler waves a pack of cigarettes in front of my face.

"Hey, Kyle. Wanna cigarette?" he asks. He knows I quit years ago, but he's intent on teasing me. My anxiety is slowly climbing, and there's nothing I'd rather do than smoke the whole pack. I'm angry about my hand and nervous for the show. I look at the clock and tell myself, "You'll be done in two hours."

I go to get my costume in the men's wardrobe room. On my spot, labeled "Froman," hangs my only costume for the night—a light blue leotard, light gray tights, and white socks. When I return to my noisy dressing room

Megan LeCrone.

(which now smells of every kind of food), I climb into my costume in my superstitious way. Tights are almost impossible to get into once I've started sweating, so I almost always warm up in costume.

Upstairs on the fourth floor, the girls of *Square Dance* are getting nervous. Many have had looks of dread on their faces throughout the day. As much as my body hurts dancing this ballet, I can't imagine what their feet feel like afterward. *Square Dance* involves a lot of fast pointe work for them, and it can be intimidating.

With my costume on, and my hair and makeup done, I make my way to the stage level. There's still an hour before the show starts, so only a few dancers are here. I sign myself in on the call board to let everyone know that I'm here for the show before starting my warm-up with some stretches.

I hope *Square Dance* looks good tonight. Rehearsal time was stretched thin this season because so many new ballets needed to be choreographed. We've put *Square Dance* together in three and a half hours total.

The New York City Ballet dances around fifty ballets per season, and getting them ready is a monumental challenge. With new ballets being put out onstage every few days, rehearsal time is in demand. This furious rush to get ballets together has always been one of the best parts about dancing here. When I first joined the company, I was impressed by how mentally challenging NYCB dancers' jobs were. Being able to learn a ballet and perform it just in a few hours goes with the territory. It makes working here like a Balanchine ballet: rehearsals are concise, with no wasted time. There's never sitting around, and if you're in the corps, you're constantly dancing. Performances have a quality of spontaneity, and dancers are in the moment because they're on their toes (in more ways than one).

"Ladies and gentlemen. This is your half-hour call. Half-hour to the top of

Adrian Danchig-Waring.

Ashley Laracey, Jennie Somogyi, and Rachel Piskin help Sterling Hyltin adjust her tutu.

Square Dance." The stage manager makes the announcement, then asks everyone to sign in. This is my cue to start my barre. I want to be warm, but I don't want to exhaust myself.

Some dancers hardly do anything before shows. They barely stretch their calves before they're out onstage. I don't understand it, but they feel they're still warm from their day. My body would break if I tried that.

The stage crew has just arrived. They mop the stage down with ammonia while I dab the sweat off my made-up face. A piano is rolled back to its corner, its driver carefully maneuvering through dancers stretching in splits.

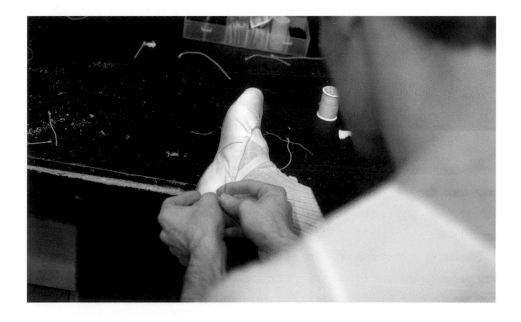

Andrew Veyette secures his shoe before a performance of Balanchine's Agon.

Rachel Piskin, dressed as a butterfly from Balanchine's A Midsummer Night's Dream, *sews a pair of shoes offstage.*

The twenty-five men shout back and forth as they screw the legs of the wings into the stage and lower the backdrop scrim. They climb ladders to adjust the lights as the girls change into their costumes. The backstage area is in full swing.

The barre space on both sides of the stage is getting more crowded with every passing minute. As I continue with my warm-up, the sweat starts to pour off of me. I watch the girls over at the rosin box. They look so glamorous in

OPPOSITE
Wendy Whelan dons her Cage *wig.*

their stage makeup and earrings, but it's funny seeing them sit on the rosin-caked floor barefoot as they prepare their pointe shoes.

The crossover hallway behind the stage echoes with the cacophony of banging pointe shoes. The girls strike their hard shoes against the wall to soften them, which makes them quieter onstage. The sound always makes me nervous. My body knows from past experiences that performance time is getting closer.

Sean Suozzi warms up for "Soldier" from Balanchine's The Nutcracker.

Lauren King, Glenn Keenan, and Ashley Laracey onstage before Balanchine's Brahms–Schoenberg Quartet.

My partner, Pauline, walks over to me. "Hi, Handsome," she says. I kiss her cheek, and her perfume envelops me. The "Onstage" call has just been heard, which means we have five minutes before the curtain goes up. The stage lights are on, and the stage is now another place, an icy-blue world.

"Can we try the pique arabesque?" she asks. Pauline always wants to try this. It's a simple step, but if both partners try to lead, it doesn't work.

We make our way out onstage. We're both ready to get going, and our nerves are annoying us both. "Now, let me turn you. Also, careful with my fingers. Marika says they're sprained."

Pauline looks at me with a grin on her face, as if to alert me to the absurdity of the situation. We both laugh as we mark through the step. "I can't grip you hard with that hand, so the lifts may feel a little different. They'll be fine, though," I assure her.

We wish each other "Merde" (the dancers' version of "Good luck"), then separate to strip off our warm-ups. The stage manager announces "Places" to everyone, but the cast of *Square Dance* is using this last minute to the fullest. All around me are girls practicing échappés and men jumping.

The stress of a hard ballet brings people together. It suddenly doesn't matter if you've been in the company ten years or two months; the experience of being naked onstage together unites us. I sometimes say "I love you" to my fellow dancers before we run out onstage for something hard. Partly for good vibes between us all, partly in surrender to the beauty of what we do. It's suddenly about ballet again, not politics, personalities, or age.

Aaron Severini centers himself by playing the piano before Balanchine's The Nutcracker.

PLEASE DO NOT MOVE THIS PIANO

DOING SO WILL DAMAGE THE DANCE FLOOR. IF YOU REQUIRE A CHANGE IN THE POSITION OF THIS PIANO PLEASE CONTACT THE PROPS DEPARTMENT AT X8846

THANK YOU

*The lights being tested
before a performance of
Robbins's* The Cage.

"Merde, everyone!" I yell to the cast onstage. The younger dancers seem
flattered, and some of them return the good-luck wish. The friendship may
be lasting or may end when the curtain comes down, but for now we're all
joining together to create something. We finalize our opening positions as the
audience begins applauding the entrance of conductor Maury Kaplow.

A hush settles over the audience and the dancers onstage. The stage
manager's calls are the only thing we hear. "House lights out—go. Curtain
warmers out—go. Curtain—go!"

SHOWTIME

*Wendy Whelan is lifted
during* After the Rain.
*Choreography by
Christopher Wheeldon.*

WHEN KIPLING HOUSTON RETIRED FROM THE COMPANY
a few years ago, the gifted soloist said something that
stayed with me. "It was never about the tendus," he said. For all
the work dancers do during the day, the reason we do it is that
short time onstage. Nothing I've experienced in life is like it,

*Janie Taylor and
Damian Woetzel in*
Afternoon of a
Faun. *Choreography
by Jerome Robbins.*

and that scares me. When I can't dance, what will ever make me feel so alive, so in the moment? When I once told a friend that I didn't pray, he said, "Your performance is your prayer. That's what you're doing up there." He was right. Whatever God is, I feel close to God when I perform.

When the curtain goes up, a gust of cold air hits us onstage. Like

OPPOSITE *A hive
of dancers from* The
Cage. *Choreography
by Jerome Robbins.*

A crew member fans the flakes, creating the blizzard onstage during The Nutcracker. *Choreography by George Balanchine.*

someone opening a window in a stuffy room, there's suddenly air to breathe, and the effect is euphoric. The change in temperature, together with the lights, is startling. You suddenly feel as if you're on another planet. The curtain of the New York State Theater has risen in silence, and the dancers are runners waiting for the starting gun to be fired.

Jason Fowler and Teresa Reichlen perform Episodes. *Choreography by George Balanchine.*

OPPOSITE   *Marika Anderson, Gwyneth Muller,*
and Saskia Beskow in Movements for Piano and
Orchestra. *Choreography by George Balanchine.*

Symphony in Three Movements. *Choreography by George Balanchine.*

A single violin breaks the stillness as two girls at the front of the stage start the dance. The strings are the first to be heard from on this program, and they're singing Vivaldi. As the rest of the corps joins in, so does the rest of the orchestra. The genius of Balanchine.

The boys dance their girls in a circle. It's our first traveling step, and it feels good to move. There's an excitement I can feel tonight in the corps. We're all so aware of one another, we feel like one.

Sébastien Marcovici and Maria Kowroski in Agon. *Choreography by George Balanchine.*

Concerto Barocco. *Choreography by George Balanchine.*

Wendy Whelan and Charles Askegard in In Memory of . . . *Choreography by Jerome Robbins.*

Brahms-Schoenberg
Quartet. *Choreography
by George Balanchine.*

As the principals make their entrances, our community onstage is complete. Sébastien is the leader of the boys, quite literally in many of the steps,
and Miranda is a princess among the girls. Their presence sparkles.

Halfway through the first movement, the corps does an exhausting series
of soutenue turns. The more tired I get, the more I wonder how my body

looks. We're all basically naked out here, but what I'm most concerned with are my legs and feet. This ballet is all about clean technique, and though it's stylized it's also very academic. Legs have to be straight and feet pointed. I couldn't care less about the rest.

It's amazing how safe dancers can feel onstage. Though we're on public display, some very private moments happen. These can be with the people we're dancing with or with ourselves.

Symphony in C.
Choreography by George Balanchine.

I'm always amused by how much dancers talk onstage. This can range from a few encouraging words to your partner to whole conversations about anything, mostly during "Party Scene" in *The Nutcracker*. It certainly adds to that surreal feeling onstage. Dancers can't admit to themselves that they're being watched by so many people. Talking reinforces the cocoon around them.

Certain performances will stay with me forever. Dancing in the Acropolis, in the outdoor theater of Herod Atticus, was magical. I danced the second movement of *Symphony in C* under a full moon,

In Memory of . . . *Choreography by Jerome Robbins.*

Fearful Symmetries. *Choreography by Peter Martins.*

with the Parthenon lit up above me. I felt lucky to be out onstage, and I knew it would be a performance that would stay with me forever. How many dancers have gotten to perform such a wonderful ballet in such a spectacular setting? The audience sat on stone stadium seats, and, since the theater has perfect acoustics, nothing since has compared to the sound of their applause.

I loved dancing with my twin brother, Kurt. The "Jockey Dance," from *Bournonville Divertissements* and our tap duet from *Duke!* were moments when

Charles Askegard and Wendy Whelan in Symphony in C. *Choreography by George Balanchine.*

Damian Woetzel in a performance of A Suite of Dances. *Choreography by Jerome Robbins.*

just the two of us held the stage. Those performances made me realize how far we'd come in just a few years.

After the energetic opening, my calves start to cramp toward the end of the first movement. Thankfully, the corps gets to leave the stage for a few minutes during Miranda and Sébastien's pas de deux. Maury draws out the final notes of the first movement as the corps boys sit their girls on their knees. Pauline and I look into each other's eyes. "That was good," I manage to breathlessly grunt. The audience seems to share my opinion, as they give us a nice hand before we escape offstage. When we enter again, we're going to be out there pushing for a good ten minutes, so I make this time count by stretching my calves against a wall and grabbing a sip of water.

Because we can't see the audience, I sometimes imagine who's out there. Instead of dancing to blackness and stage lights, which is basically what we see, I think of the different types mixing in the house. I know there's always a group of students from the School of American Ballet, but I imagine society ladies dressed to the nines, young couples experiencing ballet for the first time, and devotees who've come for years. They all see different things in the show. The ballet students notice technique, while the longtime attendees notice the quality of the performance.

Some come for the glamour of the evening, and others want to see sweat. Wherever these people have come from, their world is as exotic to us as ours is to them. Imagine wearing a suit and tie to work instead of tights. Wouldn't it be weird to wear one set of clothes all day instead of changing over and over? Do "normal" people worry how their feet are pointing?

The pas de deux continues as the corps rests in various positions offstage. Tomorrow's schedule has just been posted on the bulletin board, and dancers

Assistant stage manager Mika Melamed Hadani, Megan Fairchild, and Elizabeth Walker watch Balanchine's Symphony in C *from offstage.*

scramble to their feet and flock to it in the remaining minutes of our break. I normally wait until I'm through dancing. If I'm disappointed by what I see, it could ruin the show for me. No one else seems to be bothered by it. The minute that schedule goes up, there's a mob of dancers in front of it.

As the corps reclaims the stage and the principals exit, the audience always gives them applause. I always pretend that they're clapping for me because I've come onstage again—a private joke with myself.

The "Boys' Dance" is exhausting. It always starts out easy, but it's packed

OPPOSITE *Elizabeth Walker and Amanda Edge watch from the wings.*

with jumps. The last half of the dance is a battle with myself. My body wants to stop, but my brain keeps saying, "Push, Kyle. Push." By the end, the corps boys and principal man are spent. This is the feeling of exhaustion that makes me dread *Square Dance*.

The girls take our place while we catch our breath on the sides, still onstage. You'd think having a chance to rest would be better, but it's not. Now all the boys' calves are filling up with blood and cramping. They feel so

Rachel Rutherford stretches in the wings during Balanchine's Concerto Barocco.

engorged that it's an effort not to let it show on our faces. Thankfully, for this ballet we can stand casually on the sides, arms akimbo, but it takes every bit of strength not to double over and pant. The audience has no idea what's behind our smiles.

We've made it through to our last exit offstage. It's Sébastien's solo, and all that's left for us is the finale. I'll be sure to keep my hands to myself this time in my turn. My fingers can't take another beating.

2 and 3 Part Inventions. *Choreography by Jerome Robbins.*

From my usual spot on the floor, I watch Sébastien attempt the problematic turns from the run-through. Maybe it's because of the orchestra, or the fact that two thousand people are watching, but the turns are perfect. Sébastien was right when he assured Peter they'd be fine. I watch as he sails through the rest of his variation and can't help but see him as a man being blown through life by the wind. It's a gorgeous variation, and he dances it well.

Occasionally, retired dancers will watch from the wings. I wonder what this must be like for them. Are they sad they're not out there dancing, or are their memories enough? I know I'll be joining their ranks in a matter of years, but I don't know how I'll react. What can take the place of all these

Troy Schumacher watches Tschaikovsky Piano Concerto No. 2 *from the wings. Choreography by George Balanchine.*

performances? The lights? The applause? These days I try to see things differently; I never think, "Let's get this show over with." Pretty soon, all I'll have are my memories of this place.

Before the finale of *Square Dance*, I always rev myself up again by thinking of Merrill Ashley as the lead. I first saw the ballet on tape, and she was the lead. I've never forgotten her in it. Always a technically clean dancer with unbelievable speed, Merrill was perfect for *Square Dance*.

Thinking about that first impression of the ballet, and her, always gives me energy to finish.

The corps enters with confidence. We're ready to end this ballet. I attack my turns and jumps with everything I have. The orchestra sounds magnificent. Anticipation builds as the tempo gets faster and the steps keep coming. I look over the stage and everyone is smiling, the dancers onstage and the dancers watching in the wings. I imagine the audience is smiling too. I have Vivaldi in my ears, Merrill in my head, and Balanchine in my body. I'm in heaven.

A performance, from offstage.